How to Draw Dragons Like a Pro

A Step-by-Step Guide for Beginners to Drawing Dragons

By Leo Glasso

Copyright Page

Table of Contents

Introduction

Attention, young adventurers, and creative minds! Are you ready to embark on a fantastical journey that will unlock the power of your imagination? Welcome to "How to Draw Dragons Like a Pro," a magical workshop designed just for you! In this extraordinary adventure, you will learn the ancient art of bringing majestic dragons to life through the power of your own imagination. From fiery breath to shimmering scales, you will discover the secrets to designing your very own legendary creatures. With the help of expert guides, you'll explore the realms of fantasy and learn how to sketch, paint, and sculpt your magnificent dragons using various materials and techniques.

But it doesn't stop there! Throughout this thrilling journey, you will also embark on thrilling quests, solve riddles, and engage in exciting challenges that will test your creativity and problem-solving skills. So, grab your imagination and get ready to soar through the limitless skies of creativity. Unleash your inner artist, and let's create majestic dragons together! Get ready for a world of endless possibilities and unimaginable fun!

Character 1

Step 1

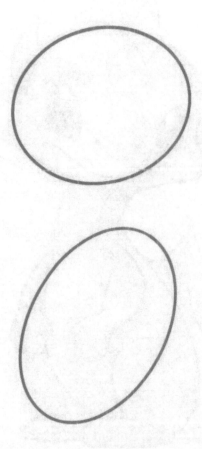

Begin by sketching two ovals as a guideline.

Step 2

Next, draw the shapes of a dragon's head and torso elements as depict.

Step 3

Next, draw the circles for the eyes and shade in the pupil as shown.

Step 4

Next, draw the curves on the head as in thick lines.

Step 5

Then, refine the curved lines to form the head as depict.

Step 6

Continue to add the lines of the ears as shown.

Step 7

Then, add the lines to refine the torso as depict.

Step 8

Next, add the lines to form the hand as depict.

Step 9

Continue drawing the lines for the lower section of the legs as shown.

Step 10

Then, add the curved lines of the wings as shown.

Step 11

Then add more curved lines to form the tail as depict.

Step 12

And sketch the lines to the face and torso as details.

Step 13

Lastly, erase any guidelines before finishing the dragon. As necessary, redraw any outstanding drawing lines.

Finish

Finally, color the dragon as guideline.

Character 2

Step 1

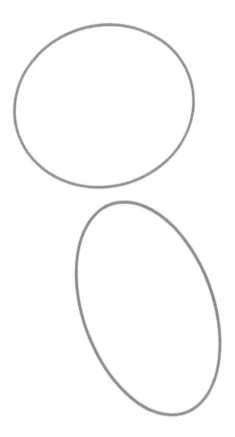

Start by drawing a head and depict the bottom part of the torso as shown.

Next, draw the curves that will connect the ears and feet at the torso for the

section.

Step 3

Next, shade the eyes with the little circular shape and give a smile to the face.

Step 4

Now, add the curved on the head as shown.

Step 5

Then, outline the lines to refine the head as guideline.

Step 6

Continue to add more curved for the ears as depict.

Step 7

Then, add the lines to represent the torso as depict.

Step 8

Then, draw the shapes of the dragon's hands as depict.

Step 9

And continue to add the curved lines for the legs section as depict.

Step 10

Now, draw the lines of the wings to the torso as depict.

Step 11

Then, draw the lines of the tail as guideline.

Step 12

Add the lines to represent the characteristics of the dragon whole body as

thick lines.

Step 13

Lastly, erase any guidelines before finishing the dragon. As necessary, redraw any outstanding drawing lines.

Finish

Finally, color the dragon as guideline.

Character 3

Step 1

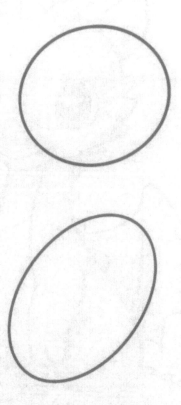

Begin by drawing two circles as shown.

Step 2

Then, design the shapes to link the form to the body (ears, wings, and feet).

Step 3

Continue to draw the circles for the sparkle eyes as guideline.

Step 4

Then, draw the curved lines for the hairs on the head as shown.

Step 5

Then, refine the lines of the head as depict.

Step 6

Next, draw the shapes of the horns on the head as shown.

Step 7

Now, draw the lines to the torso for more detail in thick line.

Step 8

Then, draw the shapes of the hands as depict.

Step 9

Then, outline the lines to form the legs portion as depict.

Step 10

Next, draw the curved lines for the dragon's wing as guideline.

Step 11

Then, draw the curved form of tail as depict.

Step 12

Continue to add the shapes of the spikes on the dragon back as thick lines.

Step 13

And draw the lines for the dragon's torso and characteristics.

Step 14

Lastly, erase any guidelines before finishing and add in a little more detail to the drawing.

Finish

Finally, color the dragon as guideline.

Character 4

Step 1

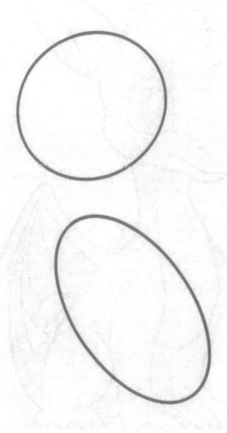

Begin by drawing the basic form for the head and body.

Step 2

Then, refine the shapes for the depict of the body component as shown.

Step 3

Next, add a smile to the face and the pupil to the smaller circles within the eye.

Step 4

Then, draw the curved lines to form the hair as shown.

Step 5

Then, add the curved lines to form the head as depict.

Step 6

Now, add the shapes of the dragon's ears on the head as guideline.

Step 7

Next, draw the lines to the torso as depict.

Step 8

Continue to add the shapes of the legs to the torso as depict.

Step 9

And add more shapes of the rear legs portion as depict.

Step 10

Then, add the shapes of the wings of the dragon as shown.

Step 11

Next, draw the lines of the dragon tail as guideline.

Step 12

Continue to add the shapes for the spicks to the rear as shown.

Step 13

Then, add features to the dragon torso by adding the lines as guideline.

Step 14

Lastly, to complete the dragon, erase the drawing lines and round the shapes, as depicted in the sample.

Finish

Finally, color the dragon as guideline.

Character 5

Step 1

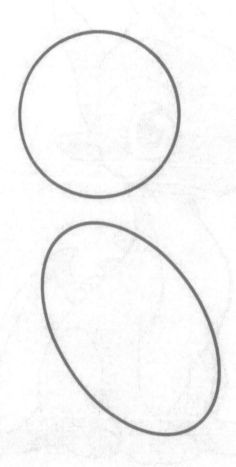

Start by drawing two ovals in thick lines.

Step 2

Next, add the forms for the ears, torso, and legs as shown.

Step 3

Then, draw the outline for the lovely eyes and add the lip on the head.

Step 4

Next, draw the shapes on the head as shown.

Step 5

Then, refine the lines of the head as depict.

Step 6

Next, outline the shapes of the ears as depict.

Step 7

Now, draw the lines of the torso as depict.

Step 8

Continue to add more curved lines to form the legs as depict.

Step 9

Then, add the shapes of the rear legs section as guideline.

Step 10

Then, add the shapes of the wings on the dragon torso as thick lines.

Step 11

Then, outlines the lines of the tail as depict.

Step 12

Now, design the shapes for more spike detail on the body as indicated.

Step 13

And sketch the line to the body and torso as details.

Step 14

Lastly, erase any guidelines before finishing and add a little more detail to the drawing.

Finish

Finally, color the dragon as guideline.

Character 6

Step 1

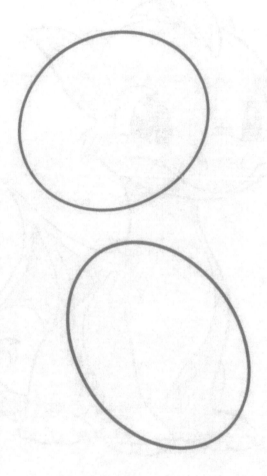

Start by drawing a head and depict the bottom part of the torso as shown.

Step 2

Next, draw the forms which form the ears, torso, and feet at the section's torso

Step 3

Next, shade the eyes with the circular shape and give a smile to the face.

Step 4

Continue to add the curved lines for the hairs as depict.

Step 5

Then, refine the lines of the head as depict.

Step 6

Then, add the shapes of the ears as guideline.

Step 7

Then, add the lines to create the hands and torso portion as depict.

Step 8

And add more shapes of the rear legs as guideline.

Step 9

Next, draw the lines of the wings as depict.

Step 10

Then, for the tail, draw the shapes as depict.

Step 11

Add the lines to the dragon's whole body as shown in thick lines.

Step 12

Lastly, to complete the dragon, erase any guidelines before finishing.

Finish

Finally, color the dragon as guideline.

Conclusion

In conclusion, "How to Draw Dragons Like a Pro!" is a thrilling and magical step towards unlocking the limitless power of your imagination, my young friends! By embarking on this creative journey, you have the incredible opportunity to breathe life into majestic dragons of your own making. Remember, imagination is like a sparkling treasure chest that holds endless possibilities. It allows you to transform ordinary moments into extraordinary adventures, where dragons soar through vibrant skies, their scales gleaming in the sunlight. Through this step, you have learned to believe in the power of your own ideas, to dream big, and to fearlessly express yourself. With every stroke of a crayon or the tap of a keyboard, you have discovered the joy of creating something truly unique and personal.

So, little artists, continue to unleash your imagination, for it is the key that unlocks the door to worlds filled with wonder and enchantment. Let your dragons fly high, reminding us all of the magic that lies within each and every one of us. Keep dreaming, keep creating, and never forget the incredible power that resides in your imagination!

Made in United States
Troutdale, OR
03/06/2024

18229493R00058